For Reese
and
Whittaker.

BUILD IT

by
Laura Seitz Danielsen

Illustrated by Michael B. Putman

BUILD IT
Text Copyright © Laura Seitz Danielsen
Illustrations Copyright © Michael B. Putman

Published June 2019 by
Legacy Bound
5 N. Central Ave.
Ely, MN 55731
1-800-909-9698
www.legacybound.net

ISBN 978-0-9904014-8-3
Library of Congress Control Number:
2019933633

All rights reserved. No part of this book shall be reproduced in whole or in part, in any form or by any means, electronic or otherwise, including photocopying, recording, or by any information storage or by retrieval system now known, or hereafter invented, without permission from the publisher.

Printed in the USA.

Join us for a day of
construction fun,
to learn about our team
and how a building gets done.

Put on your hard hat,
slide glasses on your nose.
Wear your gloves and boots
to protect fingers and toes.

First, meet the excavator,
an impressive rig.
Its main job
is to dig, dig, dig.

The dump truck carries
a really big load.
The flagger keeps her safe
as she journeys down the road.

The dozer pushes dirt
after the operator checks his oil.
The roller rumbles along
to compact the soil.

Clearing and grading -
the site is complete.
Now, the mixer can come
to pour the concrete.

The big steel beams
are made in the shop.
Then a mighty crane
lifts them up
to the top.

The iron workers
balance high
in the air,
framing the
building with
great care.

SAFETY
IS JOB
ONE!

Watch the scissor lift go
from the ground to the sky,
which helps the welder
reach places too high.

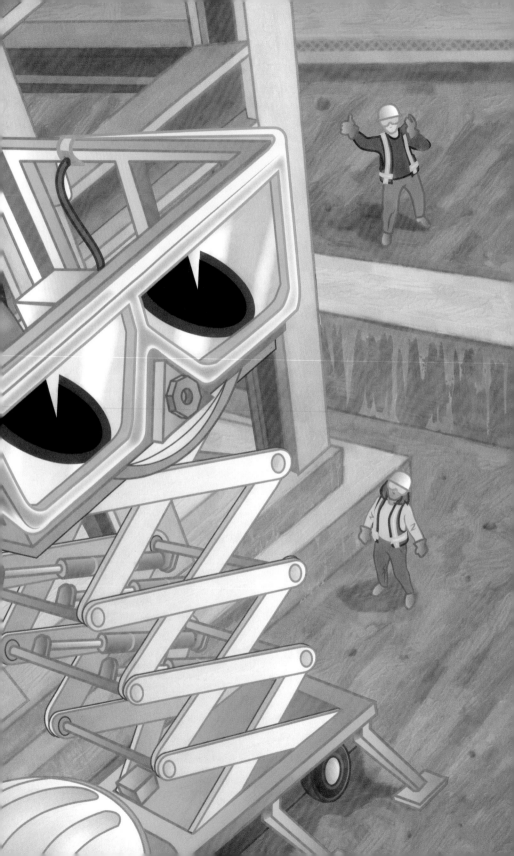

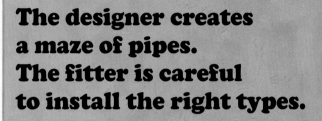

The designer creates
a maze of pipes.
The fitter is careful
to install the right types.

The job trailer holds
all the tools we use -
drill, hammer, wrench,
nails and screws.

Trade by trade and floor by floor - a building goes up where there was nothing before.

Here comes the inspector to test the alarm.
It makes loud noises to keep us from harm.

Stadiums, bridges
hospitals and schools;
we create amazing things
with our skills and
our tools.

As the sun sets on the site,
a sense of pride is instilled.
Because a team of
great leaders is really
what we build.

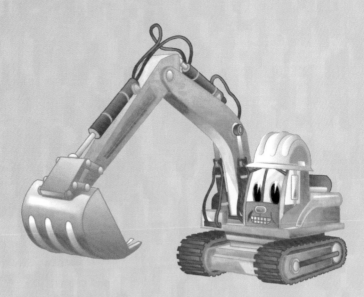

Laura Seitz Danielsen

Laura works for a construction company and is passionate about inspiring young people to pursue careers in the industry. BUILD IT is her first publication. However, she has leveraged her clever rhyming skills to win various contest and prizes, including her wedding package. She graduated from the University of Minnesota Duluth, where she fell in love with Lake Superior. She now calls Northern Minnesota home with her husband, daughter, and son. Her mission in life is to embrace adventure and to instigate fun.

Michael Bower Putman

Michael has been a "professional" artist since he was 13 and drawing caricatures at children's birthday parties. A Twin Cities based graphic designer and illustrator with 20 years of independent practice at www.putmanillustration.com, he is thoroughly enjoying moving into the realm of illustrating children's books. He hopes this colorful trip through the world of construction sparks imaginations and curiosity about how the world is built.
"Measure twice and cut once."

LEGACY BOUND

Legacy Bound is an independent
Minnesota company centered on
family. We believe that kids are
our greatest legacy. Our mission
is to offer products that help
shape children into leaders and
encourage them to explore,
imagine, and create.
For more information, visit
legacybound.net or check
out our social media pages.